Helen Keller

A NEW VISION

Tamara Leigh Hollingsworth

Consultants

Timothy Rasinski, Ph.D.
Kent State University

Lori Oczkus
Literacy Consultant

Maggie Jacoby
Helen Keller International

Based on writing from
TIME For Kids. *TIME For Kids* and the *TIME
For Kids* logo are registered trademarks of
TIME Inc. Used under license.

Publishing Credits

Dona Herweck Rice, *Editor-in-Chief*
Lee Aucoin, *Creative Director*
Jamey Acosta, *Senior Editor*
Lexa Hoang, *Designer*
Stephanie Reid, *Photo Editor*
Rane Anderson, *Contributing Author*
Rachelle Cracchiolo, *M.S.Ed., Publisher*

Image Credits: cover, p.1 akg-images/
Newscom; pp.26, 48 Alamy; pp.2–3, 16, 32, 35
(top) Associated Press; p.34 Corbis; pp.7, 11,
12, 13, 17, 21, 23 Courtesy of Perkins School
for the Blind, Watertown, MA; pp.28, 30, 31,
36 Courtesy of the American Foundation for
the Blind, Helen Keller Archives; p.19 (bottom)
Getty Images; pp.6, 7 (both), 24, 35 (bottom),
39 Time & Life Pictures/Getty Images; pp.8,
15 (bottom) The Granger Collection; pp.5,
10, 14, 20, 22, 25 Library of Congress; pp.29,
38 KRT/Newscom; p.15 (top) Picture History/
Newscom; p.18 Xinhua/Photoshot/Newscom;
pp.33, 43 ZUMA Press/Newscom; pp.40–41
Timothy J. Bradley; All other images from
Shutterstock.

Teacher Created Materials

5301 Oceanus Drive
Huntington Beach, CA 92649-1030
http://www.tcmpub.com
ISBN 978-1-4333-4863-1
© 2013 Teacher Created Materials, Inc.

Table of Contents

Chapter 1

A Hopeful Heart

Imagine silence. Imagine darkness. Imagine a world without colors or laughter. This silent darkness was the only world Helen Keller knew. It was the 1800s. People didn't know much about **disabilities**. Many **deaf** and **blind** people were seen as burdens. Often, they were sent to live away from their families.

For much of her life, Keller struggled against what other people thought of her. She struggled with what she thought of herself. But in time, Keller learned to believe in herself. Even in dark and lonely moments she tried to connect with the world. Most importantly, she learned to never lose hope and to keep dreaming.

THINK LINK

- What can we learn from Helen Keller's life?
- How would you react if you were Keller?
- How do you think Keller's life would have been different if she had been born today?

Imagine silence.

Imagine Darkness.

Imagine
a world without
Colors or laughter.

This silent darkness
was the only world
Helen Keller knew.

Silence Descends

Helen Keller was born on June 27, 1880, in Tuscumbia, Alabama. Her time as a baby was fun and filled with play. But when she was 19 months old, she got very ill. She had a high fever. It took away her ability to see and hear. Her parents didn't know what to do for her. They took her to several doctors. But the doctors didn't know how to help. Keller's world became silent and dark. Babies learn to talk by watching and listening to the people around them. Now, Keller could do neither.

Keller as a young girl

Arthur Henley Keller

Kate Adams Keller

Silent Words

People use words to tell others about their hopes, dreams, and everyday wants and needs. Keller tried to move her body to help her parents understand what she wanted. For example, if she wanted ice cream, she made two motions. First she moved her hand in a circle as though cranking an ice cream maker. Then, she shivered.

The Wild Girl

Many people in Keller's family called her a wild child. Because Keller could not say what she needed, she threw tantrums. She would often lie on the floor and kick her legs. She wouldn't let people hug or try to comfort her. She didn't trust that people wanted to help her. Keller once wrote that when she was little, she felt like she was living in a "no world."

Medical Mystery

Today, we use medicine to keep germs away and treat illness, but in the 1800s, people often became **impaired** after being sick. There weren't many medicines to help people. Sometimes, people needed to have an **amputation**. Other times, they might become deaf or blind. Hundreds of years ago, these impairments meant people could not work or care for themselves. Today, these difficulties do not stop people from living amazing lives.

Today more than 70,000 Americans are both deaf and blind.

children's ward at a hospital during the Civil War

Brain Fever

Keller's doctors called her illness *brain fever*. Today, doctors think she may have had **scarlet fever** or **meningitis** (men-in-JAHY-tis). For many days, her doctor and her parents thought she might die. When the fever broke, her parents were happy because they thought she was cured. But later, it was clear something was very wrong.

No Response

At first, Mrs. Keller didn't know her daughter had lost her ability to see and hear. Because Keller was a baby, she could not tell anyone there was a problem. Soon after her sickness, Keller's mother was ringing the bell for dinner, but Keller didn't turn her head to look. That's when Mrs. Keller knew something was wrong.

Alone

Keller's parents were unsure how to help her. So they often left her alone. Few people played, walked, or read with her. Keller spent the next five years feeling helpless and **abandoned**. Her world was silent and dark. She lost faith in people and became angry. Her parents felt as lost as she did. But they were **determined** to help her.

the Keller home

Meeting Mr. Bell

Keller's parents took her to visit an **oculist** (OK-yuh-list). The doctor looked at her eyes. But he said there was nothing he could do for her. However, the doctor thought she could still be helped. He told Keller's parents about the inventor Alexander Graham Bell. Bell knew about working with the deaf because his mother and wife were deaf. Keller's parents found Bell and asked him for help. He told them about Perkins School for the Blind.

Bell with Keller

Dear Anne

When Keller was nearly seven years old, her parents wrote Dr. Michael Anagnos at Perkins. They **pleaded** for his help. He promised to send Anne Sullivan. She was a teacher trained to help students like Keller. When they met, Keller didn't know Sullivan wanted to help her. In her anger, Keller treated Sullivan badly. She even knocked out two of Sullivan's teeth.

Sullivan knew she and Keller would need to have a meeting of the minds. Sullivan knew how tough life was for Keller. She was nearly blind herself. Before she became a teacher, she lived in a **poorhouse**. There, it had been hard for her to get help. She knew what it was like to feel lonely and afraid. Sullivan had attended Perkins. The doctor hoped she would be able to teach Keller some new ways to communicate.

Sullivan was the top student in her class at Perkins, but teachers called her "Miss Spitfire" because she had a temper.

Sullivan began by using her hands to communicate with Keller.

Anne's Dream

Sullivan believed in the power of education. She knew people were more likely to succeed if they attended school. Sullivan was able to attend Perkins because a wealthy man saw how much she loved school. He paid for Sullivan to attend.

Learning to Trust Again

Sullivan had to earn Keller's trust. She took Keller to live in a small house behind the Keller home. They stayed there for two weeks. There, Sullivan **enforced** rules about Keller's behavior. She was tough and patient. It was the only way to teach Keller to follow directions. She began to talk to Keller with her hands. Keller couldn't see. So Sullivan used her fingers to draw in Keller's palm.

In time, a change came over Keller. Finally, she knew Sullivan was there to help her learn. She couldn't see, hear, or talk. But Keller was very smart. Until she met her teacher, there had been no way for her to show it.

"Ivy Green," Helen Keller's house in Alabama

Laura Bridgman

Learning from Friends

While at Perkins, Sullivan learned many things from her friend Laura Bridgman. She was blind and deaf. Bridgman taught Sullivan how to communicate with people who could not speak. One of the most important things Sullivan learned was that blind and deaf people are just as smart as other people.

"I awoke and found that all was dark and still, I suppose I thought it was night, and I must have wondered why day was so long in coming. Gradually, however, I got used to silence and the darkness that surrounded me and forgot that it had ever been day."

–Helen Keller

Keller with Sullivan

15

It was at this water pump that Keller understood words were names.

One day, Sullivan and Keller were outside at the water pump. Keller still didn't know words were names for things. But Sullivan had an idea. She placed one of Keller's hands in the running water. Keller felt the cool liquid on her skin. In the palm of her other hand, Sullivan spelled the letters *W-A-T-E-R*. Now, Keller understood. She took Sullivan's hand and copied the motions Sullivan was making.

Soon, Keller learned how to speak with her hands. Keller's parents had spent years not being able to help their daughter. Now they could finally "hear" her voice. Later, Sullivan taught Keller to read and write. Many people believed it would be impossible. But Sullivan and Keller worked hard to connect with other people.

South Boston; Dec. 24, 1891.

...hands,

Surely I must ... Christmas-letter or you ... have forgotten you! ... Gardiner friends ... have been all this ... have written to you ... me? I am sure you will, for you are very kind, and when you receive this tardy little courier you will know that I love you very, very much, and that I often ...

Square Hand

Sullivan first taught Keller to write using *square-hand script*. The writing was done on a board with deep squares cut into it. The ridges guided Keller as she made boxy letters.

Keller reading

The Mystery of Language

Keller wrote about the feeling she had that famous day at the water pump. "Somehow the mystery of language was revealed to me." Keller called it a "rebirth" when she could shape the word *mother* in her mother's hand.

Braille

As Keller's skills grew stronger, Sullivan taught her to understand braille. Braille was invented by a blind man named Louis Braille in the early 1820s. Braille heard of someone in the French army who used raised dots and dashes to write in the dark of the night. Braille took that idea and made it simpler. He used clusters of six tiny raised dots to identify letters with the touch of a finger. And with his system, a blind person could write using a simple tool.

Today, braille is still used to read and write. But many people use modern technology, such as audio books, instead of reading.

This boy uses a machine that scans a book and reads it out loud through a speaker.

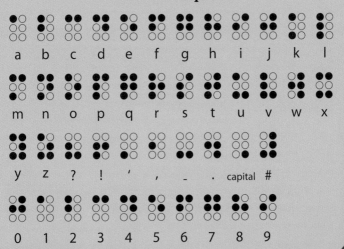

Braille Alphabet

a	b	c	d	e	f	g	h	i	j	k	l

m	n	o	p	q	r	s	t	u	v	w	x

y	z	?	!	'	,	_	.	capital	#

0	1	2	3	4	5	6	7	8	9

Louis Braille

Use the Braille alphabet to read the message below.

19

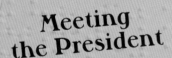

Chapter 2

A New Life

Many were amazed by all the things Keller could do. Stories about her and Sullivan appeared in newspapers. When Keller was eight years old, she was invited to Boston. Keller traveled by train with her mother and Sullivan. She had never left home before. She was curious about what the world looked like. Sullivan spelled words in Keller's hands. She described everything she saw as they traveled.

Meeting the President

On this same trip, Keller traveled to the White House to meet President Grover Cleveland. He had heard of the wonderful ways Sullivan was helping Keller and wanted to meet them in person.

President Grover Cleveland

Learning Abroad

In the 1800s, many people who studied disabilities lived in Europe. Over 40 years before Perkins was founded in America, educators built schools for the deaf and the blind in Europe. Many of the teachers from Perkins were trained in Europe.

Perkins Institution for The Blind, Watertown, Mas

Perkins was home to the largest collection of braille books in the United States.

The Perkins campus in Boston.

When they arrived in Boston, they went to Perkins. This was the school where Sullivan had studied. All the students at Perkins were blind or deaf. Sullivan and Keller spent three winters there. Each time, they were able to learn new things. Keller was excited to explore the school's library. She studied many subjects like geography, math, and French. But her greatest joy was to find other children who also used finger spelling.

A New Way to Talk

Keller wanted to learn to talk. Young children learn by listening. They **mimic** the sounds they hear. Keller was never able to listen to people speak. But she believed if she and Sullivan tried, together they could find a way for Keller to learn to talk.

When Keller was 10 years old, they asked a woman named Sarah Fuller to help. Fuller had traveled to Europe to learn ways to help blind and deaf people. She taught Keller to use her hands to listen. She touched the speaker's lips, tongue, and throat. Keller used her fingers to "see" the person's lips moving. And she used the **vibration** from the throat to "hear" what was being said.

Keller used Fuller's technique to "see" and "hear" a child speaking.

Sullivan spoke into a recording machine to help Keller learn to speak.

Never Giving Up

Keller was never able to speak as clearly as people who learned by listening to others. It was a great disappointment to her. However, she never stopped trying to make her speech better.

DIG DEEPER!

Finding Her Voice

Keller used a variety of methods to communicate with the world. She was determined to make her voice heard and to understand what others were saying.

Reading Lips

Keller sometimes relied on her own form of lip reading. She used her left index finger, middle finger, and thumb to touch people's nostrils, lips, and throats to understand words.

Keller "listened" to singers with her hands. Her right hand marked the beat.

Finger Spelling

Sighted readers don't read letter by letter. They read each word as a set of letters. Keller understood fingerspelled words the same way. She didn't interpret letter by letter. She understood each word separately.

"Miss Fuller's method was this, she passed my hand lightly over her face, and let me feel the position of her tongue and lips when she made a sound. I was eager to imitate every motion and in an hour had learned six elements of speech: M, P, A, S, T, I. I shall never forget the surprise and delight I felt when I uttered my first connected sentence: It is warm."

—Helen Keller

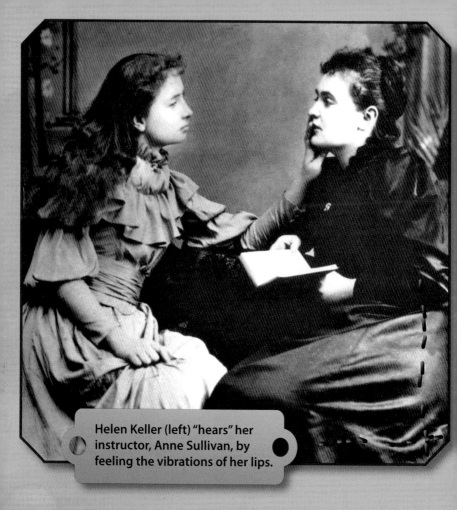

Helen Keller (left) "hears" her instructor, Anne Sullivan, by feeling the vibrations of her lips.

Doing the Impossible

Keller was eager to go to college. Her family didn't have as much money as they once did. And she wanted to take care of herself. To be accepted, Keller knew she would have to pass many tests. At 16, she went with Sullivan to Cambridge School for Young Ladies to prepare. Many people liked Keller. But some thought her disabilities would keep her from getting into college.

Cambridge was an **intimidating** place. Keller had never been to a school with students who could see, hear, and talk. She was treated like every other student. Keller needed more time to do the work than other students. But she worked with Sullivan. And Keller passed her college-entrance tests with honors.

Finding the Right Books

Early on at Cambridge, Keller and Sullivan couldn't find books in braille. This meant Sullivan had to shape every letter of every word into Keller's hands. It was exhausting for both of them. Today, there are laws that require braille books to be available for students.

Learning More

When she entered school, Keller wrote these lines in her diary:

"I find I have...things to learn in my school life here—and indeed in life—to think clearly without hurry or confusion, to love everybody sincerely, to act in everything with the highest motives..."

Keller was accepted into Radcliffe College. She loved reading and writing. English was her favorite subject. Keller's teacher suggested she write for a magazine. She started by writing simple stories about her life. She wrote about her struggles, about Sullivan, and how she learned to be herself. People loved the stories. In 1903, Keller's articles were made into a book. And people all over the world read it.

RADCLIFFE COLLEGE.

CERTIFICATE OF ADMISSION.

CAMBRIDGE, July 4 1899.

Helen Adams Keller

FRESHMAN Class in Radcliffe College.

Agnes Irwin
Dean of Radcliffe College.

passed with credit in Advanced Latin.

Harvard or Radcliffe

When she was a little girl, Keller told Sullivan that she would one day go to Harvard. But in 1900, women weren't allowed to go to Harvard. Instead, they were admitted to Radcliffe, a sister school. Both Sullivan and Keller felt as if Keller had accomplished her dream when she was accepted to Radcliffe.

Keller's acceptance letter to Radcliffe

In 1904, Keller graduated from Radcliffe. She and Sullivan walked across the stage together to accept the **diploma**. The crowd cheered so loudly that Keller could feel the vibrations. She had done what many people told her was impossible. No one thought a child who couldn't hear, see, or speak could become anything. But Keller had graduated from college. And she had become a **published** author.

Strong Headed

Once someone asked Keller why she chose to go to Radcliffe. She joked, "Because they didn't want me at Radcliffe and, being stubborn, I chose to override their **objections**."

Chapter 3

Telling Her Story

Keller loved Sullivan very much. Sullivan was the woman who had helped Keller escape from the dark world she had once lived in as a child. Keller never wanted other young people to feel as alone and out of control as she had felt. For many years, Keller and Sullivan traveled around the country giving lectures. They showed people how they could speak to each other with their hands. People told Keller that even though she was different, she could still make her dreams a reality.

Living Together

Keller used the money she earned from her book to buy a house for Sullivan and herself. She told Sullivan that she wanted to "devote [my] life to those who suffer from loss of sight."

Keller and Sullivan's house

Keller, Sullivan, and Macy

Sullivan Marries

While at Radcliffe, a man named John Macy helped edit Keller's biography. He and Sullivan fell in love and married in 1905. Macy knew how important Keller was to Sullivan. The three of them moved in together and lived as a family. Unfortunately, the marriage did not work out.

Forever Friends

As Keller became an adult, all kinds of people were interested in her story. In 1918, she and Sullivan went to Hollywood. A movie about Keller's life was being made. They were pleased with it. But the movie was too dramatic for their taste. Keller and Sullivan decided to tell the world the true story. They traveled the world together and met with many people.

In time, both women grew older. They stopped traveling and rented a small house on the beach. Sullivan's health grew worse and worse. She died October 20, 1936. Keller was at her bedside, holding her teacher's hand.

Chaplin with Thomson, Keller, and Sullivan

New Companion

Keller and Sullivan hired Polly Thomson to travel with them. Since Sullivan and Keller worked without breaks, there was no time for them to do chores. Thomson was hired to help Keller and Sullivan stay organized.

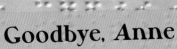

Keller and Thomson at home with their dogs

Goodbye, Anne

Sullivan's health had been failing for a long time. But she loved being with Keller. She told Keller, "I am trying so hard to live for you."

Books and Movies

In her lifetime, Keller published more than 10 books. As an adult, she traveled across the United States and around the world. She even starred in a movie about her life.

1903: *The Story of My Life*
1908: *The World I Live In*
1927: *My Religion*
1929: *Midstream: My Later Life*

1938: *Helen Keller's Journal*
1955: *Teacher: Anne Sullivan Macy*
1957: *The Open Door*

In 1955, Helen received an Academy Award for the documentary about her life.

Keller's passport

meeting with young fans

Helen's World

Many people loved Keller's beautiful writing in *The World I Live In*. Keller told how she experienced the world through smell, taste, and touch. She wrote about how she used her hands to "see" the world. And then, when she learned to communicate with people, she saw the world through the words people used. In the book, she said she felt just as good about her life as people who could see and hear.

Final Days

When Sullivan died, many people thought Keller would avoid public life. But Keller knew Sullivan wouldn't want that. Instead, Keller continued to travel the world, bringing hope to the blind. It was the same hope Sullivan had brought her.

When Keller grew older, she could no longer travel. In 1961, Keller had a **stroke**. She spent the rest of her life writing and reading in her home. On June 1, 1968, Helen Keller died. Even though she was never able to see or hear, nothing stopped her from enjoying life. She loved to learn and to explore. And she refused to let anything stop her from following her dreams.

High Praise

In 1964, Keller received one of America's highest honors. President Lyndon Johnson awarded her the Presidential Medal of Freedom. The award recognized her work to help the blind and handicapped.

Helen's Highlights

Keller traveled to 39 countries during her lifetime. Today, Helen Keller International continues Keller's work. Keller co-founded this **nonprofit organization** that works to prevent blindness around the world. Below are some of Keller's favorite places she visited.

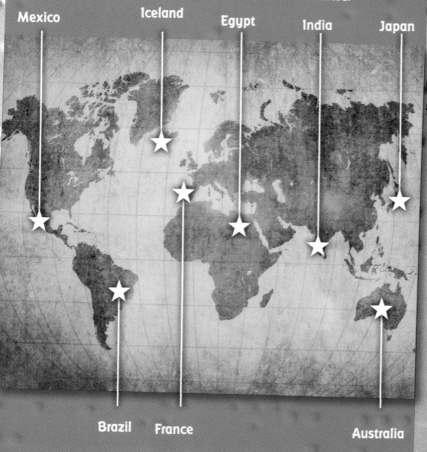

Mexico
Iceland
Egypt
India
Japan
Brazil
France
Australia

A Living Legacy

Keller's **legacy** of helping people is still alive. Helen Keller International works to prevent blindness and improve nutrition. Camp Helen Keller offers a six-week summer camp for blind children. Children are free to play games, make crafts, swim, and dance. Helen Keller Services for the Blind offers a variety of services and programs for all ages. One is the Louis Anzalone Braille Center, which is a major producer of braille textbooks. Through her legacy, Keller's dream remains strong. And she continues to show the world new ways to see.

"The best and most beautiful things in the world cannot be seen nor even touched, but just felt in the heart."

–Helen Keller

Keller with the actress Patty Duke, who played the young Helen onstage and in the movie *The Miracle Worker*.

Time Line of Helen Keller's Life

1880
Keller is born in Tuscumbia, Alabama.

1882
Illness leaves Keller blind and deaf.

1887
Sullivan arrives.

1888
Keller takes her first trip to Perkins.

1896
Keller attends Cambridge School for Young Ladies.

1900–1904
Keller attends Radcliffe College.

1902
Keller's articles are published.

STOP! THINK...

- What do you admire most about Keller?

- Why do you think Keller spent so many years attending school?

- What kind of life would Keller have had without her teacher Anne Sullivan?

1903
The Story of My Life is published.

The Story of My Life
Helen Keller

1904
Keller graduates from Radcliffe.

1962
The film *The Miracle Worker* opens.

The Miracle Worker

1936
Sullivan goes to the hospital where she later dies.

NEWS
HELEN KELLER DIES

1968
Keller dies.

Glossary

abandoned—to be left alone without help

amputation—to remove a body part because of illness or injury

blind—to be unable to see

deaf—to be unable to hear

determined—strongly committed

diploma—a document showing that a person has graduated from school

disabilities—the lack of abilities or power to do things completely or at all

enforced—made someone obey a rule or a law

impaired—to not work perfectly

intimidating—scary or frightening in a way that makes someone question his or her ability to do something

legacy—something handed down from the past

meningitis—a disease in which the brain or spinal cord becomes infected

mimic—to copy

nonprofit organization—an organization that uses its earnings to support a good cause

objections—reasons for not wanting or liking something

oculist—a doctor that specializes in eyes

pleaded—begged

poorhouse—a place where orphans and people who can't pay their bills live

published—to have written articles or books that are
  available for many people to purchase and read
scarlet fever—a disease that includes fever, pain in the
  nose, throat, and mouth, along with a red rash
stroke—a medical condition caused by a blocked or
  ruptured blood vessel in the brain; may cause loss of
  feeling, loss of muscle use, or even death
vibration—rapid motion back and forth; a trembling
  motion created by sound waves

Index

Bibliography

Cottin, Menena. *The Black Book of Colors.* **Groundwood Books, 2008.**

Experience this book with your fingers instead of your eyes. The illustrations are made with raised lines and are accompanied by written text as well as braille letters.

Davidson, Margaret. *Louis Braille: The Boy Who Invented Books for the Blind.* **Scholastic Paperbacks, 1991.**

Learn about the man who invented braille, the alphabet for the blind, at just 15 years old.

Garrett, Leslie. *Helen Keller: A Photographic Story of a Life.* **DK Children, 2004.**

This book is full of photos, facts, and quotes about Helen Keller's life. It also includes a photographic time line of events.

Gibson, William. *The Miracle Worker.* **Scribner, 2008.**

This play show's Keller's life as a student, with Sullivan as her translator. This drama has been performed in schools and theaters around the world.

Smith, Kristie. *Dottie and Dots See Animal Spots: Learning Braille with Dots and Dottie.* **iUniverse, Incorporated, 2007.**

Want to learn braille? You can learn how to read the braille alphabet through two characters who travel to the zoo and see braille letters and words.

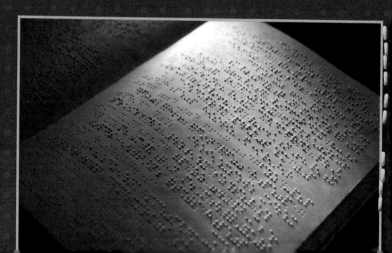

More to Explore

Garden of Praise
http://gardenofpraise.com/ibdkell.htm

This website includes an easy-to-read biography of Keller's life as well as games. At the bottom of the page, you'll find a seven-minute video with footage of Helen Keller.

Helen Keller Kids Museum Online
http://www.braillebug.org/hkmuseum.asp

This website is part of the American Foundation for the Blind's website. It has lots of photographs of people and places that were significant in Helen Keller's life.

Ivy Green
http://www.helenkellerbirthplace.org

Explore Keller's birthplace through photographs, floor plans, and maps. If you're in Alabama, you can take a tour!

Kids Konnect
http://www.kidskonnect.com

This website has a brief biography. It also provides over two dozen links to related websites. To learn more about Keller, click on *Alphabetized Index* at the top. Click on *K*. Scroll down and click on *Keller, Helen*.

Neuroscience For Kids
http://faculty.washington.edu/chudler/chtouch.html

These 16 experiments will give you a chance to focus on using your sense of touch, instead of hearing or sight, to identify objects.

About the Author

Tamara Leigh Hollingsworth was born and raised in Cupertino, California. She attended Hollins University, where she earned a degree in English. She has been a high school English teacher for many years. She currently lives in Atlanta, Georgia. When she is not working with her beloved students, Tamara loves to spend time with her husband, her daughter, and her books—especially biographies.